Selected Poems
1967–2011

George Jonas

Selected Poems
1967–2011

With an Introduction by
Margaret Atwood

Cormorant Books

Copyright © 2015 George Jonas
Copyright Introduction © 2015 O.W. Toad
This edition copyright © 2015 Cormorant Books Inc.

No part of this publication may be reproduced, stored in a retrieval system or transmitted, in any form or by any means, without the prior written consent of the publisher or a licence from The Canadian Copyright Licensing Agency (Access Copyright). For an Access Copyright licence, visit www.accesscopyright.ca or call toll free 1.800.893.5777.

  Canada Council   Conseil des Arts
       for the Arts   du Canada

   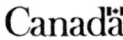

The publisher gratefully acknowledges the support of the Canada Council for the Arts and the Ontario Arts Council for its publishing program. We acknowledge the financial support of the Government of Canada through the Canada Book Fund (CBF) for our publishing activities, and the Government of Ontario through the Ontario Media Development Corporation, an agency of the Ontario Ministry of Culture, and the Ontario Book Publishing Tax Credit Program.

LIBRARY AND ARCHIVES CANADA CATALOGUING IN PUBLICATION

Jonas, George, 1935–
[Poems. Selections]
Selected poems, 1967–2011 / George Jonas ; with an introduction by Margaret Atwood.

ISBN 978-1-77086-475-7 (paperback)

I. ATWOOD, MARGARET, 1939–, WRITER OF INTRODUCTION
II. TITLE. III. TITLE: GEORGE JONAS.

PS8519.O5A6 2015   C811'.54   C2015-907872-5

Cover design: angeljohnguerra.com
Interior text design: Tannice Goddard, Soul Oasis Networking
Printer: Sunville Printco

Printed and bound in Canada.

CORMORANT BOOKS INC.
10 ST. MARY STREET, SUITE 615, TORONTO, ONTARIO, M4Y 1P9
www.cormorantbooks.com

Selected Poems
1967–2011

CONTENTS

Introduction   1

From *The Absolute Smile* (1967)

Peace	7
In Any City	9
Public Parks	11
Portrait: The Freedom Fighter	12
Four Stanzas Written in Anxiety	13
Tuesday, June 28	14
Temporal	16
Eight Lines for a Script Girl	18
Memories	19
Four Stanzas for the Authorities Who Wish to Know My New Address	20
Six Stanzas on Homesickness	21
Five More Lines	22
Song	23

From *The Happy Hungry Man* (1970)

The happy hungry man	24
I will resist	29
Epitaph for a Spanish Peasant	30

God pardons some	32
Moses and I	33
It is quite possible	34

From *Cities* (1973)

A Love Poem	35
The Girls of Whitney Hall	36
Landmarks	38
City Elegy	39
Greenwich Village	42
Park Avenue	43
Garment District: A Pilot Speaks	44
Queens Plaza	45
Carnegie Hall	46
Amen House	47
Warship on the Thames	48
Lady on the Avenue of the Virgin Mary	49
Air Raid Rhymes	50

From *The East Wind Blows West* (1993)

Inscription	53
Father: A Portrait	55
Nocturnal	56

From *The Jonas Variations: A Literary Seance* (2011)

Near the Beloved	58
Fallaci in Milan	59
Poet on the Gallows	62

In Homage	63
The Falcon Song	65
A Meal in Charleroi	66
I Don't Remember …	67
Second Evening Song	68
Misery Dreams	69
Consciousness	70
The Town	74
Autumn Day	76
Ibn Ammar Al-Andalusi, 1000 A.D.	77
To a Fascist Deputy	79
Sea Breeze	81
Rebirth	82
Acknowledgements	83
About the Author	85

INTRODUCTION

GEORGE JONAS — ACERBIC JOURNALIST, libertarian political commentator, mordant crime writer, risk-taking radio and television producer, forger of witty epigrams, erudite multilingual reader, motorcycle enthusiast, indiscreet raconteur, wearer of black leather garments, loyal friend to his friends, loyal annoyance to his enemies — this George Jonas, who has worn many guises and played many parts, began, in my own life, as a poet.

This was in the Sixties. Faced with the plummeting of reliable sales of *Hamlet* as high schools moved away from the set curriculum, Jack McClelland of McClelland & Stewart had begun his policy of aggressively publishing Canadian authors. Meanwhile, younger writers — most but not all of them poets — were sensing a dearth of opportunity for their literary works, and were forming new companies: Coach House Press, Talonbooks, and House of Anansi among them.

Anansi put out its initial list in 1967. Among its titles were a reprinting of my own first book, *The Circle Game*, and George Jonas's first collection, *The Absolute Smile*. So I knew George in the way poets knew one another then: we published in the same small literary magazines, we collected in the whirls and eddies around the public poetry readings that had sprung up here and there, we helped edit one another's books, and we read one another avidly: a new poetry collection was an event among us.

I seem to have known George by letter even before I met him in person. (We wrote paper letters then, depositing them in mailboxes, with stamps on the envelopes.) The contact was made through Dennis Lee, a mutual friend and poet and soon to be the co-founder of Anansi. It was George who suggested that I submit work to *Kayak*, a poetry journal operating out of Santa Barbara, not then the upscale address it has become. Sure enough, there is *Kayak*, listed on the Acknowledgements pages of each of our books.

Then I myself got sucked into the vortex of Anansi, becoming at first an unofficial poetry editor, then an official one as well as a board member.

And so it was that I met George. It must have been around 1969; miniskirts were still with us. George was already sporting the tinted glasses that remained his trademark; he was smoking some recherché kind of cigarette; he had a thin tie, being, not then and not ever, a person who went in for hippie *déshabillé*. What an elegant figure he cut!

He would have been right at home in the fin de siècle of Whistler and Wilde, in the eighteenth century of Pope and Swift, and possibly among the steampunkers of today. But not, for instance, among the romantics of the Keatsean variety: not for him the dreaminess, the open shirt, the windblown cravat. His excesses were of a different kind. Byron would be a fitter comparison: the combination of world-weariness, edged quips, and dollops of here-today gone-tomorrow sex, plus the odd tender love lyric — that was closer to the Jonas style. Some years later, George was on a writerly junket in the Northwest, and was boarding a plane; one of the writers commented of his fellow passengers that these were not the people he would choose to die among. Came the Jonas drawl: "When it comes to dying, it doesn't much matter who you do it with."

George was not exactly of his time, or rather the time in which I met him. He was older than my cohort of young poets, having been born in 1935, as opposed to our 1939, 1940, and 1941. He was extra-sophisticated: not only was he European, with the advantage that conferred in those days before "Eurotrash" had become a term, but he had escaped from Hungary during the 1956 uprising — an uprising that had occurred while I was still in high school, and that had made a deep impression on me. How daring! Such an escape granted him extra points, and the right to be amused by the naïveté of innocent Canadians like myself. I was later to meet other members of the Hungarian diaspora who had made it to Canada and distinguished themselves in the arts — Anna Porter, née Szigethy, who became a publisher of mine; John Kemeny, film producer; George Kaczender, film director — but George Jonas was my first. They all knew one another, and shared a certain kind of knowledge, and a certain kind of darkness.

So there was I, a naïve, miniskirted Canadian, and there was George, amused. George was later to commission a teleplay by me. That was in the early 1970s. The play was called *Grace Marks*, and was the story of the double murder that took place in Richmond Hill in the 1840s described by Susanna Moodie in her second book, *Roughing It in the Bush*. This play would lead to my 1996 novel, *Alias Grace*. But none of this was known to us while George and I sat at an outdoor café on — as I recall — St. Clair Avenue.

At that moment I was somehow supposed to be editing George's second book of poetry, *The Happy Hungry Man*. I recognize the jacket copy I wrote for the back of the book: I was a dab hand at writing jacket copy in those days. "Jonas interrogates a contemporary life," I wrote. "What is real when a man has food and hence no belief in food? When he has shelter and hence cannot pursue it?... what is at stake in his recent poetry is our lives."

Not bad, as jacket copy. But I don't recall that I did much actual editing. George's work was already finished. In fact, it was already polished. I may have suggested something about the order of the poems, which form a quasi-autobiographical sequence (think Byron's *Don Juan*). But that was about all I did.

How fresh these early poems seem today! Direct, formally accomplished, restless, incisive; conscious of death and history and of the meaninglessness of much human activity, but conscious also of fleeting moments of pleasure, and not immune to love. These poems are devoid of self-pity even when they speak of it. Jonas spares no one and nothing, but especially not himself.

> Wearing a braided tie,
> Cheerful most of the day,
> I write poems as I
> Have almost nothing to say,

Jonas quips of himself in his poet persona. Those of us who have read his poems over the years — not to mention his other writing — don't believe him, however. He has had a great deal to say. And he has said it, always excellently.

Margaret Atwood
Toronto, November 2015

PEACE

I wish to make a positive statement
Of happy hunters returning from the woods.
Wardens of dwindling flocks, serious concern
Dwells in their moist and beautiful eyes.

There is no conflict that love or bullets
Could not resolve in time.
Gardens are carefully planned. Long rows of roses sit
In all directions around any house.

There is always a period of peace
Between two blows, when a smiling landscape
Surrounds with blue light the resting warrior.
The raised arm hardly shows among the ferns.

At such times rabbits jump out of their trenches
And stand listening at the entrance of the field.
Worms pop out of the ground in open amazement,
Sharp-beaked birds freeze unfalling in their dive.

The moment is guarded by dustbins along the streets
Of low and crippled suburbs where later
Children come out of hiding and women pause for breath.
Hate, suspended, sways gently back and forth.

Rats are pacing the floor, thinking,
A loaf of bread cuts itself into warm slices,

A glass of milk travels to India,
Warships lean on their guns and close their eyes.

The beauty of such moments is hardly useful
Except for the purpose of missing a heartbeat,
As old men sit at tables, ready to talk.
For there is nothing to talk about.

IN ANY CITY

In any city at any hour of the day
We pray.

With narrow, calculating eyes
We are getting off streetcars in front of churches.
Not too far from stock markets and parliament buildings
We attempt to placate God
By giving pieces of candy to filthy children.
Generally
For each ten men we destroy
We restore one;
For each dollar we extort
We return a nickel to the priest
And a penny to the poor.

Luckily our God is a Jew
A shrewd kindly old Jew who knows his children well.
Our way of doing business is his way.
His motto too is live and let live
And a little honest profit is all he expects
On which to keep his Kingdom going.
A slight depression now and then cannot be avoided
In his difficult line.
If he can make us do our bit
And be in some vague fear of him all the time
He is satisfied

                                                                         [...]

And in the end he opens for us
The gates of his heaven.

Of course, there will be a few even he cannot help.
A few who are unable to find a place in this soap opera of a world.
Misfits, who are not at home, no matter what,
In this fat, happy, cause-and-effect, give-and-take universe,
A few vicious saints who want all or nothing.

These lost souls are out of the reach of God.
He cannot give them all because he too has to stay in business
So he gives them nothing.
With a sad flick of his beautiful patriarchal finger
He sends them flying after a while
Into the outer darkness.

PUBLIC PARKS

The grass of which I am thinking grows in public parks
Even after they had been turned into cemeteries
Or black, skinny trees that compete for the attention of passersby
After the war with the neighbourhood theatres.

The city belongs to the sparrows, and I alone
Know at times who the sparrows belong to
But I am bound by oath never to tell.
I lost my watch by these bushes one year.

The eleventh soldier had been exhumed
Approximately six months after the siege
For two more hours he lay exposed in a hole by the taxi-stand
The drivers look at him quite solemnly at first.

I think one sees any city in a different light
After discovering that the bottoms of overturned streetcars
Are reasonably bulletproof, though one should never
Be more than fifteen feet from the nearest doorway.

Now the season of light rain on green leaves,
Cool peacefulness and hesitant sunlight
Lies outside of my window over a strange,
Over a deceptively familiar public park.

PORTRAIT: THE FREEDOM FIGHTER

In the streetcar conductor's uniform
The man tried to roll himself a cigarette
Without letting go of his machine gun.
"It's a dog's life," he said, scratching himself with satisfaction,
"Rotten war," he said, viewing with deliberate pleasure
The hulk of a burned-out streetcar among the torn cobblestones,
"Want a fag, kid?" he asked me, being an elder
For the first time in his life among his passengers.
Later the night came but he did not go to sleep
In the cool mist and total darkness the city belonged to him
"It will be a long time before we mop up the bastards,"
And he waited for approval and reassurance.
The barricades ran half way across the square,
When he turned his eyes toward me I hesitated to answer,
He looked at my face but he was looking at my skull.

FOUR STANZAS WRITTEN IN ANXIETY

The museums and stock markets protect me
Orchestras hold up naked swords in my defence
The steps of a melancholy policeman at midnight
Echo down my quietly segregated street.

My unguarded wealth rests inside the cold walls
Of silent court houses and libraries
Where after seven o'clock the lights are dimmed.
Narrow electric eyes patrol my jewellery stores.

I am fair, peaceful and wise; my smooth voice
Is never raised; I forgive and forget
My grey navies sit in heavy waters,
My compassionate guns are trained at the world.

But lately the mornings are sudden
Odd noises in my innermost rooms.
They who sidestep my books and bayonets
Worship stones, I hear, and need no beds to sleep in.

TUESDAY, JUNE 28

I wonder if there will be room for both of us
In this poem.

I have explored you as far as my fingers would take me
And you are nowhere.
Perhaps you invite so lightly
Their expedition through your body's regions
Because you know:
Fingers can't reach you.

Aimlessly, like an iceberg
You float on
With most of what you are immersed
In jealous depths of yourself
A tip above the surface showing
To photograph, to dress and to destroy.

I will stop searching for you, I will
Pretend that I have found you: you are
Easy enough to see, to feel, to touch.
I will allow your tongue to flicker
In and out of my ear, your lip
To circle my lap, and not remember
You are only doing your duty and have no hope
Of pleasing even yourself.

I will stay with you
Until the wind blows you away.

Whenever we meet
After our ritual is over
I will incline my head and listen
For the silence between your breasts.

TEMPORAL

This is one of those Tuesdays
I want to be old.
Then you will be old too
For I wish you a long, long life.

Sometimes I will see you in the street
As I see other old women now
Who used to be desperately desired
By all sorts of old, dead men.
It is a comfort for me to see them
And oh, it will be a comfort for me to see you.
Grey strands of crinkly hair half-hiding
Long, flat ears
Thin legs ending in knotted ankles
Shuffling in black walking shoes
A quick glance at you
From top to bottom
That's all.

If doctors still permit me the odd cigar
I will light one after each such meeting
And sit by a window overlooking a street
A crowded street, full of young, nervous girls
Hurrying to meet their lovers
As you claimed to have hurried to meet me
Climbing the stairs on what might be called the same legs
Darting quick glances of promise
Through biologically the same eyes
But refusing my hand when I reached for the hips
You must have lost in a careless moment since.

Naturally I will have no pity
And no more reason for anger.
I will marvel, though
At the handiwork of God, at the fact
That I could have spent sleepless nights on account of this body
Which we both thought was yours
A comparatively short time ago.

EIGHT LINES FOR A SCRIPT GIRL

I almost know you now. You are your name,
The substance of your skin, the movement of your eyes,
The line of your lips, the texture of your hair,
Your phone number, the colour of your voice.

You are your breasts' shape, the full length of your limbs,
You are your smile, your nail polish, your dress.
Later I'll know you more. Still later
I'll know you even less.

MEMORIES

The room has four walls, the room is empty,
and there is nothing left in the room.
Around the room the house is dying
the way worlds die.
I lived here, I am told. I don't remember.

What I remember is nothing to speak of:
a summer perhaps, and a flow of streams.
Now I am tired. Elephants
sit on my dreams.

FOUR STANZAS FOR THE AUTHORITIES WHO WISH TO KNOW MY NEW ADDRESS

I am surrounded by gentle omnipotence
I have many Wednesday evenings to pay for
Many glasses of water to empty
Many bedsheets to grope for in the dark.

I live where trucks float on turnpikes of ice
Past my impersonal windows
Where headlights explore my curtains
As I lie pinned to my bed.

Everyone has free access to my room
And after midnight they increase
I hide as they enter intent on their business
Through the revolving doors of my silence

I hide but I may still exist somewhere
Perhaps in pictures on the black leaves of scrapbooks
Perhaps in cities I have travelled through once
In the sad eyes of those with no time to kill me.

SIX STANZAS ON HOMESICKNESS

The Tower thought that I was alone
And placed himself squarely before me:
"*Now* what do you do?" he said
Happy, that I was not amused.

"I am with my friends," I murmured,
"Tower go away, go away.
You mean nothing to them at all.
This is something purely personal."

I closed my eyes, not that it helped.
"Tell them about me," the Tower sat down.
I was embarrassed for who would care
To bore his new friends with an old Tower.

"We were children together," I blushed.
"I can't turn him out, can I?" I whispered.
Unbidden shadows crossed the room
My friends looked at me with some concern.

"His first stones were laid in the tenth century,
He really is an interesting old Tower,
I saw him every day, going to school.
Maybe he has something important to tell."

But my apologies were all in vain
My friends' eyes grew cold and seemed to turn inward
And I thought Towers must mean more than friends
But then he left quietly, I never saw him since.

FIVE MORE LINES

I speak a language I have never learned,
I do not belong to any nation,
I hurl sharp poems at the world
And keep looking at the wounds in my skin
At their point of penetration.

SONG

I am thirty-one
Described as a man
I want to be alone
And it looks as though I am.

Coming from the tribe
In which angels abide
I always told the truth
When I thought I lied.

Now with features pretty
And with powers dark
I live in the city
That grows in my heart.

Wearing a braided tie,
Cheerful most of the day,
I write poems as I
Have almost nothing to say.

I own a fountain pen,
A car with bucket seats,
And share a young woman
With two dead-end streets.

This Saturday I will
Lean on her well-shaped thighs
Wondering how I'll feel
In 1985.

from THE HAPPY HUNGRY MAN

                      The happy hungry man believes in food
                      The happy homeless man believes in a home
                      The happy unloved man believes in love
                      I wouldn't mind believing in something myself.

Wakes up in   Look at rocks
a good mood   Rocks look back at you
one morning   Stare at water
                    Water stares
                    You can play endlessly
                    Dropping words one
                                    by
                                          one
                    Until you fill the pit of silence
                    Or adding up seconds
                    Until you reach the sum of time
                    You can also sit down and eat
                    Lie down and sleep
                    Stand up and whistle
                    There is the air to breathe in and fly through
                    There are hills to climb up and look down from
                    You can build houses too
                    And destroy them
                    Beget children
                    And sprinkle gasoline over their bodies
                    You can learn foreign languages

Dolce far niente
Arbeit macht frei
And take strange women for long walks
In beautiful afternoons
You can make up codes for your friends
Secret signals of sounds
From bars of indifferent music
You can broadcast your voice
And televise your face
Or grow very old and ugly
There is simply no end to all the things
You can do.

Sometimes one is almost tempted to go on living.

Walks through a park on his way to work

We all have
A bench in the park to reach
And some of us reach it.
I saw an old man this morning who did.
He seemed to be happy.

Green, black and brown were the predominant colours,
The sky threw in some blue, the clouds some white.
He himself was pink.

He held a stick in his hand, a safeguard of some sort
Against gravity, dogs, the universe,
The dangers of existence, his own buckling knees,
All known enemies inside and outside,
Even perhaps the Angel of Death.

Well, a stick is better than nothing.
He must have been eighty, he must have known
All fights are unequal
Otherwise how could there be victors?

Sitting among modest flowers
A kind of victor himself
He raised his eyes to follow my progress.

Tries to decide where to spend the night

Sleep only with strangers
    for strangers sleep in peace
And will be perfect hosts
    you being a perfect guest
May touch nothing of yours
    and you nothing of theirs
Except their outer skin
    And the coffee pot in the morning.

Sleep only with strangers
    for they are open and kind
They know you are here today
    and gone tomorrow
If you carry away a little object
    they can spare it
If you leave one behind
    they can throw it out the next day.

Be a knock on the door
    a voice on the telephone
The promise of a postcard
    without a return address
Sleep only with strangers
    it is for you they reserve
Their freshest linen
    and their cleanest smile.

Calls a girl

Come,
Let us make a date to die
Tomorrow after dinner.
We could have a quiet meal, at Tony's perhaps,
Then go to my place and cut our wrists.

If we did that we might retain
(Not you me or me you, that's not important)
But that which otherwise always passes.
Wouldn't it be a change to belong forever,
Like lesser people, not to each other
But to ourselves as we are?
What's the point of motion
When there's nowhere to go?
What's the point of growing
When we end up not containing ourselves?

Instead of more promises, mere resolutions
To haunt us, kept or broken,
Come, let us simply die
In a mutual moment
Asking/offering
No commitment.

**Sits in a
small craft
approaching
a landing strip**

　　　　　　　　　　I will resist
The temptation to lament
The passing of my youth, the loss
Of many certainties, the gain
Of two sorrows for each anger,

Instead I will note a little of the slow
Movement of objects along a slender
Line between the gently rising
Breasts of two firm hills across

The approaching land, the parting
Lips of a ravine, the erection
Of trees, the capricious glint
In the cold eyes of a nameless lake.

At the library, sees an old newspaper clipping of a poem by Attila Jozsef side by side with a picture of Lorca

Epitaph for a Spanish Peasant

General Franco called me up to wear the
    uniform of his soldiers
I might have run, but was afraid he'd catch me
    and have me shot
So I took up his arms and fought well
    against Liberty and Justice
At the wall of Irun, and seem to have died
    just the same.

Epitaph for a Spanish Poet

It may have had to do with the love
Lovers felt for you that
You had to be killed.
The blind struggle continues without you
You are not necessary to it
There will be other causes now
There will be other poets.
In this picture, your corpse looks indifferent
O Federico Garcia!

Recalls lunching with an executive of the Canadian Broadcasting Corporation

                        Being
Vaguely upset by the fact
That even the very sparrows perish,
They pulled some strings, sent me on a mission.

I met God yesterday.
He sat on a sort of throne
We were both slightly embarrassed.
"I have no answers for you," he said finally.
I was relived but tried not to show it.
I had no questions.

                         God pardons some
But they lead aimless lives,
Hear their names whispered at unexpected hours,
Their hearts beat visibly and their lovers
Fail to recognize them in the street at times.

They dare not be by themselves as they're always alone,
They tend to rise early but are usually late,
Their laughter seems too ready, their smile too remote
Indeed, it is better not to be forgiven.

Because God's mercy is colder than liquid air
And those he permits to punish themselves will learn
To envy the crosses and the crowns of thorn
The Father keeps for sons particularly dear.

Later he sits at a conference where people accuse him of being cynical

                    Moses and I
Must have climbed different mountains
Or must have been advised by a different god
For look at the writing on the stones in my hand:

It seems I may not respect my parents
Or my neighbour's right to the things he believes
    he owns
Or the lives of those I consider to be my enemies.

Before you begin to envy me
Remember only this:
My god's bidding is as remote from my nature
As your god's is from yours
And I find his commandments
As difficult to keep.

That his circle narrows

It is quite possible
That our common thoughts come to us from the sea
Our doubtful soul follows the herrings
And we all die after the 11 o'clock news
Still there is
A certain self which I for my part
Keep wrapped in tinfoil among my private papers.

I am less and less concerned
With a planet I share with Arabs and caterpillars
With a country I share with fellow motorists
With women who share me with film directors
And with a heart that after minor adjustments
Could be used by a customs officer.

The trips I will take from now on
Must only be a few inches in length.

A LOVE POEM

May I tell you the truth?

When I dropped the sailboat's anchor
on the skull of the fish, its mouth opened wide
but only in agony, not supplication
as knowing no mercy pikes ask for none;
but fighting well for a body of fourteen
pounds of muscle and slippery green skin,
pulling a deep-keeled boat a quarter of a mile
surviving a keen slap of the paddle between the eyes,
a pair of pliers drawing a three-pronged hook
out of its gullet, taking whatever came with it,
and still biting the fisherman's finger with three rows
of immaculate teeth set in its dead jaws

may I tell you the truth —
cover girl   without eyelashes   lipstick
I saw your face.

THE GIRLS OF WHITNEY HALL

Let me compose a simple prayer
    for things beyond recall,
embracing in the gentlest terms
    the girls of Whitney Hall.
No insight, bitterness or wit,
and soft enough to whisper it
    behind a private wall.

God, all they ever asked for was
    some perfect happiness:
marriage, orgasm, status, fame,
    free access and egress
for which in rooms they roamed a lot
talking of T.S. Eliot —
    why should life give them less?

The girls of Whitney Hall remain
    still pictures in a scene.
Textbooked, tennisballed, telephoned,
    progressive, poised and keen.
Married, fat, sucked up in a fog,
(one even coupled with a dog)
    unchanging and serene.

Please, God, give them wings to fly
    and suntanned legs to walk;
poetry, sweet pain, requiems,
    and small suburban talk.
Life insurance and ecstasy,
a blue Mercedes by the sea:
    the flower and the stalk.

Because they are now 30 and
    perceive the shadows fall;
because they've all held hands with Death
    in brief ways, shy and small;
they're still desired by some men,
their hairdressers remember them,
O God absolve them if you can:
    the girls of Whitney Hall.

LANDMARKS

After sixteen years I remember you
Ossington bus, O'Leary Avenue.

Perhaps gravity makes them loom so large
West Lodge, St. George Street, York garage.

Northcliffe backyard, where cops used to appear
after midnight to confiscate my beer

or Glenholm boarding house, five bucks a room,
whose dome languidly crumpled into doom

and bursting water pipes had drowned in steam
the ex-mate of a German submarine.

The beanery on Queen Street where a lame
girl first sat in my booth and asked my name.

Or long before, a metal winter night,
a funeral home's sign casting a light

flickering blue on grey December slush:
with cardboard trunks, torn clothes, needing a wash,

an evil-smelling strange boy, tall and thin,
had asked to spend the night. And god knows why

they took me in.

CITY ELEGY
for Dennis Lee

The sky is pink tonight
from 300 feet
a penthouse vista over Toronto
a tailgunner's vista
the sky is pink tonight
      a radius of 7 miles
a perimeter of 22
a blue bell touching
the dark fringes of the lake
flashes of white   yellow strings
streaming slow-motion headlights
but on the horizon where it matters
the sky is pink
          They say
pink skies mean war   War
the ancient Lancaster sleeping
in the waterfront's most peaceful park
dreaming of night skies over London
      Vienna   Budapest
remembering a crossbeam of searchlights
dumping its load   another street exploding
beneath the baleful shadow
an older architecture crumbling
before the ultramodern shape
      now on a pedestal
sleep   ancient Lancaster   sleep
      Pink skies mean war
they say   pink skies mean war

maker of all cities   war
destroyer of all cities   war
reason behind all cities   war
under the safe sky of Toronto
this sprawling peaceful city
the ancient Lancaster and the scribe
fellow-travellers   old enemies   proud
      naturalized citizens
think of war: father   creator
preserver of cities   war
     yes: it is not
skyscrapers   subways   green belts
theatres   neighbourhoods   children
but war that forges a city and no city
lives that has not lived through war
and only bricks and people made concrete by blood
add up to a city and without Mackenzie's
cabbage patch there would be no foundation
for the skyline of the city of Toronto
and without it the fastest growing city withers
and wishing it were not so is only wishing
     of why
do our best citizens rail against America that gives us
nothing but peace prosperity and void:
     the price of peace.
If the City Council's aim is joyful musicians
let it support the symphony: if it's music
it must support the Air Force
                 Yet
saying it   knowing it to be true

is to be sad beyond measure
Better penthouses
pink skies   illusions
                              blue bells touching
the dark fringes of the lake

GREENWICH VILLAGE

The girl who shares this upstairs room
with a cat, a guitar and a chesterfield
left her native town, Sarnia,
because it was the end of the world.

First she moved on to Montreal
then crossed the ocean to Prague,
quickly returned to Los Angeles
and now she's bitterly crying.

She's bitterly crying I suppose
because she'd seen much sea and land
without once having glimpsed that world
of which Sarnia is the end.

PARK AVENUE

When the middle-class girl and I
were finally lying side by side
on the white rug of her living room
in an expectant mood and naked

"What would you like me to do?" she whispered.

I admit her question surprised me,
it only seemed appropriate
for a virgin or a prostitute
and I did not think she was either.

In fact she turned out to be both.

GARMENT DISTRICT: A PILOT SPEAKS

No ribbons, eh, some of you boys got no ribbons,
said the Air Force general,
                              spent your time
ferrying toilet paper to France in those C46s, eh?
Well I'm giving you a chance: you take off
tomorrow at 0600 with the paratroops,
cross the Rhine, hang on for 35 seconds
over enemy territory, come back to base,
then get your asses over to the office
and pick up your ribbons. Don't wet your pants,
I'll be right there with you.

And so he was: at 20,000 feet
in an armour-plated B27,
while we lumbered in at 600
and were picked off by flak and small arms fire.
Of forty C87s four made it back to base.
Yes, we got our ribbons
ten days before the war was ended.
                              Mind you
I suppose the Rhine had to be crossed
and one of the surviving pilots was run over
by a milk truck later in the States.
I don't know what happened to the other two.
I'm in business for myself now, making ribbons.

QUEENS PLAZA

Here is where the elevated line
goes underground
                        quite legally.
My neighbours huddle closer together.

The cop who is supposed to defend us
against hippies and hoods and blacks
has just walked into our subway car
and he is hanging on.

The gun in his open holster
seems to be of the finest blue steel.
At least twice in my life before
I was glad to own such a gun myself.

Maybe I would like to have one now.
There are subways and subways,
this subway lurches wildly on its tracks
throwing the cop off balance, but not quite.

We passengers could look up and read
each other's eyes like books, but we don't look up.
Soon we will cross under the river.

                        Meanwhile
everybody is his own secret policeman.

CARNEGIE HALL

Because sadness is costly
and inadequate
        and after a while
siege guns scale down to overtures

and finally our houses become ruins or monuments

also because of the hope that there will be a mind
to remember or to forget these cities
where bodies are even now being discharged
from hospitals and morgues
                      or admitted
into offices and jails and high society
                          This is
for the explorers of ephemera

This is for students of coded words
exhumers of graves and connoisseurs of explosions
collectors of potsherds
                or readers
of the writing on the wall

This is trumpets for the ears of those whose hearing
has not become too subtle for loud music
it is kettledrums
                the rending
of foundations
              it is grenades
shattering granite

AMEN HOUSE

Prowling around E.C.4
one cannot help noticing
OXFORD UNIVERSITY PRESS
having a head office in
   LONDON
with branch offices in
GLASGOW   NEW YORK   TORONTO
MELBOURNE   WELLINGTON   BOMBAY
CALCUTTA   MADRAS   KARACHI
KUALA LUMPUR   CAPE TOWN
IBADAN   NAIROBI and ACCRA

Immediately the mind hands down
two heavy sentences
to run concurrently:

An empire *sic* on which *transit*
the sun *gloria* never *mundi* sets

WARSHIP ON THE THAMES

"In poetry there are neither big nations nor small …"
George Seferis

A poet and his lady gracefully accept
a leather-bound Russian edition of his book
from a peace-loving cultural attaché.

Small white hands hold cocktail glasses
all night long. Then like grey elephants
mansions of commerce march along the quay.

Suddenly under the deserted bridge
a claxon's blast warns of a slender
warship slicing the river in half.

The peace-loving poet carefully monitors
the braided water behind the twin screws.
Light naval guns point at his lady.

Academic eyes, sardonic, secure,
view the passing of the ship. A great navy:
a great agent for a great literature.

LADY ON THE AVENUE OF THE VIRGIN MARY

In this strange world of outer space
    vulnerable and small
she calls for her lover because
    who else is there to call?

Her nights are cold, her days are dry,
    her planets far away,
she says her love will never die,
    what else is there to say?

In this strange world of outer space
    she has no one but you:
love her. Learn to see her ways
    from her point of view.

Be faithful to her, and she'll cut
    the core out of your heart;
in one sense it is unfair but
    who else is there to hurt?

AIR RAID RHYMES

A child, very shy:
dark death, I wondered, bitter death,
painful death, why?
What is it, who
makes it, how does it come about,
is it true?
Was there someone, perhaps a survivor,
who knew?

A bomb, my teacher said,
weighs fifty pounds.
During class, from hand to hand,
a bit of shrapnel made the rounds.
Dark death, I wondered, bitter death,
painful death, why?
What is it, who
makes it, how does it come about,
is it a lie?

When walls collapsed, the bodies
were covered with burlap sheets.
Air raids were fun, school was out early,
we were playing in the streets.
I remember being a siren: I screamed,
the others ran.
I dived like a plane, like a bomb I exploded,
learning to be a man.

Wardens were digging up cellars,
the dead were laid in a row,

gas-mains burned
with a beautiful blue flame:
I was longing to know, to know.
Dark death, I wondered, bitter death,
painful death, what is it you feel?
But the faces were closed and secretive,
rigid, black, shrivelled, and sealed.

I woke at dawn, shivering, I think my
father was watching the silver darts
trailing white smoke in a pink sky.
Go to bed,
father said,
this is not an alert only a warning:
it's Warsaw they're bombing this morning.
Tell you what we'll do,
we'll put it to music for you:
"Not an alert, it's only a warning,
it's Warsaw they're bombing this morning."

My father playing the piano,
grey puffs of ack-ack sprouting in the sky,
dark death, I wondered, bitter death,
is it a game or a lie?
What is it, who
makes it, how does it come about, why?

When the sirens started up again
some bombs, my teacher said,
weighed fifty pounds;

spilling the ink, watching the purple stain.
I weighed a hundred pounds: would I be death,
if I dropped on a city from a plane?
Would I be dark, would I be bitter death,
would I be pain?
Would I be faces, cold and black and sealed,
if I were Death itself, what would I feel?

And growing silver wings, I rose, I flew,
I soared across the city, sweet and shy,
becoming Death, having no wish to die,
having no patience with my father's song,
being in air raids on the ground was wrong
and while good boys took shelter with the rest,
I rained phosphorus bombs on Budapest.

INSCRIPTION

Signals   signals
behold   from the outer darkness
another flash of light:
Cor mea clavis

The heart is my key
(to good & evil, no doubt)
the key is my heart

Breakfasted on bones
wiped my mouth with
my best friend's hand
dumped my lover   my lover
into the dustbin—
the world is safe:
Cor mea clavis

The arbiter   the judge
inside my chest   my head
my conscience   my
categorical imperative
my one-to-oneness with God
(no moderator: no moderation)
my honesty   my faith
gut-feeling   amygdala
by any other name:
Cor mea clavis

                              [...]

It opens & locks any door
such is the key of my heart
a skeleton-key

Looks perfect on a crest
in a blue field   across
a sinister bar & under
the tip of a sword

FATHER: A PORTRAIT

He dreamed at his clavier and counted his gold,
and knew instinctively it's futile
as is reading Goethe or growing old
or arguing with a crocodile,

but he took it for granted for some reason
that posterity's a valid forum,
for everything there's a season,
and Adolf Hitler would die before him.

He promised my mother, it appears,
that a Mediterranean villa
awaits the prudent man who steers
a course between Charybdis and Scylla.

But readers of Goethe learn to accept
a quirk of the world no gold can redeem:
that dreamers wreck their ships on a fact
and prudent men, on a dream.

NOCTURNAL

Oh how we entered
> dear madame dear
a temple well tempered
> oh how we entered.
Glances held four beats full
slim fingers sculptured slim
> icons with sainted
> gestures newly painted
cool nipples textured cool
all centres centred:
> > lean
invisible man: keen
woman, heads turning slowly, in
we went, skin
brushing against skin,
> oh how we entered, a drop
at a time, a stop
after each note
a flute
in his crushed velvet suit
a harp,
strings taut in her smart
Missoni coat
> but now a little fear
> strikes the hammerklavier
where, how much, through what jumbles,
snakes, bones, trinkets, truth serums, iron maidens,
whose nails
across whose eye
for that matter how soon or why:

Perhaps a lapse
perhaps a lapse again, perhaps a lie?
      Dear madame dear
with all centres centred
how well tempered
      is the temple we entered?
Now for a last brilliant passage
slim fingers on the keyboard of her spine
his eyes   crushed velvet   blue
      c'est tout.

NEAR THE BELOVED

I think of you,
   when sunset paints the seashore
a crimson hue,
and when the moon
   spreads salve on the abrasion,
I think of you.

It's you I see,
   when clouds of dust are whirling
high on a ridge,
or when I look
   at rippling waves returning
beneath a bridge.

I hear your voice
   in the rumble of thunder:
a voice I will
listen to as
   the summer nights meander
and all is still.

I'm at your side.
   No matter what the distance,
you're always near;
as stars replace
   the sun without resistance,
would you were here.

A free translation of "*Nähe des Geliebten,*" Johann Wolfgang Goethe's (1749–1832) tribute to a Romantic strain in German literature.

FALLACI IN MILAN

In this sixth year of the new millennium,
considering each measurement that matters,
the West seems in the pink; the East, in tatters.

Marx and Mao dethroned. It's rags, not riches
for ex-serfs of the great man of steel, Stalin,
whose successors excel mainly in stealing.

Self-immolating Islam curses and twitches
in its own blood, not yet having the skill
to draw much blood from others — though it's learning.

Despite the goodwill, wealth, personal valour
of some rulers, and oil in the ground,
the Levant languishes in Biblical squalour.

Time marches. The logic of the migrant
follows a path from famine to feast,
from stagnation to a life that's vibrant,
to the free West from the despotic East.

Measuring ages by a rule of thumb,
as history's relentless wheel keeps turning,
a cycle starts, a clock begins to tick,
the lean grow sensitive, the satiated numb,
the mean protest, the good don't give a damn,
and London fiddles while London's burning.

A cricket chorus of the Left that frets
unceasingly about nuclear threats
goes on to view with exquisite aplomb

the Muslim population bomb.
The word is imprecise: there's no explosion,
at least not literally, from the Islamic womb,
the process throughout Europe is erosion.
A puzzled population, getting older,
feebly looks on as Mesopotamia,
seeps through the soil, the air, the blood,
a trickle yesterday, today a flood,
mixes with Tunis, Algeria,
till those who go to sleep in France or Spain,
wake in Eurabia.

Europe having been peeled of her defences,
a big white onion, layer by layer,
the old alarm: *Italia irredenta!*
appears warranted as a muezzin calls
the prophet's vanguard camped inside the walls,
the faithful of Roma, to evening prayer.
Across the drawbridge infiltrators saunter,
with no Tancred to relieve the siege,
and only one Cassandra-clone, a sage
fool, rails by the gaping gates, to counter
rabid Arab with gilt Florentine rage.
Behind the walls huddle the moribund,
across the moat come surging the fecund.
One woman only, in white, a chic crusader,

makes a last stand for the western realm
in Rizzoli's mall between Duomo and La Scala
against a tide from the Gulf States to Ghana,
wielding a quill-shaped cudgel ... Good luck, Oriana!

    Gabriele D'Annunzio (1863–1938), popular Italian poet, novelist, war hero and enthusiastic supporter of Mussolini's Ethiopian adventure, might have written this poem about the fiery Florentine journalist Oriana Fallaci, had he lived long enough to witness her battle to preserve Italy from encroaching "Eurabia."

POET ON THE GALLOWS

Dawn stabs a bloody finger at the Seine,
Gawk and shiver, my fellow citizen.
A swig will take the chill off your pelvis:
Villon, François, poet, at your service!

As my life reaches its apogee
I offer for it no apology.
Some cobble cloying sonnets in an arbour,
I'll perform instead my danse macabre.

Familiar with hunger and with thirst
I flattered many princes, killed a priest.
At the gates of hell I will not stand alone
As the Fiend divides us, each soul to his own.

I am a Frenchman, born of the elite,
At a moment no moment shall surpass.
Paris, my city, is spread beneath my feet,
My slender neck supports a weighty ass.

> Written in homage to Francois Villon (1431–1463) and George Faludy (1910–2006), who made the poetry of the French vagabond survive into the Twentieth Century.

IN HOMAGE

1.

When Caesar crossed the Rubicon
not knowing if his luck would last
he used a gambler's metaphor:
"The die is cast."

Antiquity had forty-nine
years to go yet, after a scorn-
ful Caesar came, saw, conquered.
Then Christ was born.

Tempted, scourged, nailed to the cross
for sowing salvation's discord,
he said, in words as clear as air:
"Forgive them, Lord."

When soldiers rolled dice for his robe
heaven's sun spun into eclipse.
Man's son suffered the vinegar-soaked
sponge touch his lips.

Rome crumbled. Years marched like legions.
The earth orbited, as it must.
God raised Christ to his right and rendered
Caesar to dust.

2.

As the ponderous universe revolves
one wonders: is it all a Judas kiss?
God poses puzzles that he never solves.

Is each new dawn a yawn? Each height
>	a new abyss?

With mankind standing on the brink
of novel closures and erasures,
catastrophes are simmering.
Christ's mystery quickens the pulse.
>	So does Caesar's.

Who renders what to whom and in which order?
Does Conscience trump King, or is King the test?
Is the right word explosive? Exquisite?
Eli, Eli, lama sabachtani? Or is it:
>	*Alea jacta est?*

A tribute to the poet Heinrich Heine (1797–1856).

THE FALCON SONG
for Barbara Amiel

Hand-raised myself a falcon bird,
by year's end she was grown.
Tenderly tamed her, but she still
seemed restless, prone to roam.
Gilded her feathers carefully
especially her wing,
one day she wheeled and flew away,
snapping her silver string.

At dusk today or just before,
I saw a falcon bird.
Trailing behind, a silver string,
she wouldn't heed my word.
Gold shimmered underneath her wing
in answer to my calls.
May merciful God help restore
all disunited souls.

A variation on the theme of "*Der Falkenlied*" by the
Twelfth Century knight-troubadour known as Der Kürenberger.

A MEAL IN CHARLEROI

After eight days of exercising the soles
of my footwear, hot, ravenous, tired,
I dropped by the Green Inn to inspect the holes
in my poor pair of boots before they expired,

then, sitting anyway, I ordered some slices
of bread and butter, with garlic ham, not too hot,
all I could afford at their exorbitant prices,
and when the girl brought the plate, I ate the lot.

I was happy, and she, with huge trays laden,
as pink and white as the ham, no less tasty,
poured me a beer with verve rather than style,

her eyes on the foam. Mine were on her waist. She
seemed a kissable stout Belgian maiden,
all billowing breasts and sunshine for a smile.

A free translation of the sonnet "*Au Cabaret-Vert, cinq heures du soir*" by Arthur Rimbaud (1854–1891).

I DON'T REMEMBER...
   for Anna Porter

I don't remember how blonde was her blondness,
all I know is that fields of wheat are fair,
and in summertime's sizzling sunlight I sense
in fields of wheat, the tincture of her hair.

I don't recall the blue of her eyes' blueness,
until departing September's surprise:
deep in the whirling autumn sky's lacunas
glows the cerulean blue of her eyes.

I waited for her words to fall like manna.
I don't recall them, but when meadows sigh
in spring, I hear the gentle words of Anna
from a far-off spring, as distant as the sky.

From the *Anna-cycle* by Gyula Juhász (1883–1937) — a translation.

SECOND EVENING SONG

Recollecting in the fading waste
of dissolution, dissonance, decay
childhood enchantments of a sweeter taste,
old invitations, innocent, to play,
as when I covered your small hand with mine,
is only treading water over time.

So, too, observing old towns in decline
under flapping cloud canopies of spring,
or watching greedy seagulls wheel and climb
above foam-speckled pebbles, sunset-red,
the boulder-fringed graves of the seaside dead,
is only treading water over time.

When darker notes begin to haunt his soul
Man conjures cryptic images in white
refurbishing the landscape of his fall,
as trudging along darkening paths home,
he trails a pallid spectre. It's his own.
Swan songs only tread water over time.

    A variation on the theme of "*Abendlied*"
    by Georg Trakl (1887–1914).

MISERY DREAMS

Lush ballrooms, lounges, supper clubs,
tuxedos, crinolines,
hush, look. In some nearby slum
upon a mattress on the floor
misery dreams.

A bleak, factory-ravaged lad,
hollow-chested, he glints
as smudges of cold moisture sit
on his lips. As royal as
a sleeping prince

he dreams for himself a girl, a bowl
of fruit, both washed; a deep
dish of soup, fresh linen.
He dreams of running water, then
laughs in his sleep.

He dreams of coughing up less blood
and of the day he can afford
some meat, and dreams another year
will pass until he must appear
before the Lord.

City, pause for a few minutes,
taste not your caviar and cream,
and leave your champagne flutes unfilled.
In some nearby slum, misery
dreams its last dream.

A free translation of "*Álmodik a nyomor*" by Endre Ady (1877–1919).

CONSCIOUSNESS

Dawn separates earth from the sky,
a fissure, gentle, life-revealing,
at whose razor-sharp command
children and insects twirl into being.
There is no moisture in the air,
a sparkling lightness levitates;
during the night, like butterflies,
little leaves settled on the trees.

I dreamt of blue, red, and yellow
blotches. They amounted to order,
accounting for each speck of dust.
Sneaking across a murky border,
now order flows molten in my limbs.
The moon climbs. The day has begun
in a universe in reverse.
At night inside me shines the sun.

A thin man, I subsist on bread,
prayed for once and eaten twice,
hoping one day to throw for it
something more substantial than dice.
Rump roasts don't rub against my lips,
I am what my fortune allows.
Even the cleverest cat, indoors,
can't catch a harvest mouse.

Like a pile of split wood, the world
is heaped upon itself. At rest,
each piece squeezes, clutches, eludes,
infests and determines the next.

That which is not, will sport a bush,
that which will be, slyly increases,
that which is, is a thing of the past,
it wilts, changes colour, falls to pieces.

Inside the freight yard, flat against
a soot-sodden tree's roots, I crouched.
Strange-tasting, sharp-edged, semi-sweet
industrial weeds touched my mouth.
I kept my eyes on the guard's stubborn
shadow, as he, well-fed and tough,
kept jumping between shiny heaps
of coal. What was he thinking of?

Misery lives inside. Outside
only misery's explanation.
Wounded souls festering in fever
are easy to diagnose. Creation.
Cause and effect. Logic and order.
No one can come into his own
by cutting wood and mixing mortar
to build his miserly landlord a home.

From underneath the night, watching
revolving sky's cogwheel: a patient,
majestic loom of bygone times
weaving luminous legislation
from the delicate threads of chance
I marvelled, till past misty dreams
I noticed the fabric of the law
keeps coming apart at the seams.

Silence listened closely. The clock
struck one. My anger spent,
why not revisit youth, I thought,
the peeling walls of wet cement
where I knew freedom. And a flock
of constellations, planets, Mars,
watched me scramble to my feet.
The stars sparkled like prison bars.

Iron can weep and rain can laugh.
I heard them both. The past can split.
A man can forget, if only what
he conjures up. Life is not it.
Nature affords me no choice
I love till I run out of steam.
Why should I have to forge a sword
of you, my precious self-esteem?

A grown-up person, who at last
has learned to sit back, not to fret;
who knows: life is the appetizer
before the main course of death;
who clings to no host, parent, priest,
but drinks his soup, and then, replete,
rises politely, leaves the table,
and lets the waiter clear his plate.

I recall seeing happiness.
She was soft, blonde, and weighed a ton.
Across the implacable grass
swaying her way with great aplomb,

plunking her curly smile in a
lukewarm puddle, she called for rough
play. I still see the hesitant
moonlight fiddling with her fluff.

I live near the tracks. Trains
come and go here. When one passes
rows of bright windows disrupt
evening's fluttering semi-darkness.
That's how illuminated days
hurtle through endless night's reprise.
Lit up by each private compartment,
I lean on my elbow. Keep my peace.

A free translation of "*Eszmélet*" by Attila Jozsef (1905–1937).

THE TOWN

Monochrome sea, grey drizzly spray,
        and a town, the colour of slate,
where gables bend in slow degrees
under the fog's spectral weight,
and on the strand in briny breeze
        marsh grasses sway.

No woods nearby. No birds to sing in May.
No glint of spring. Sunlight remains a hint,
        by June it fades away.
The humid August air stays warm.
The town — damp, desolate, forlorn.
        The clouds look torn.
Harsh cries of passing waterfowl
pierce through the chilly gloom of fall,
        the days grow small.

Yet all my heart belongs to you,
fog-ridden town,
        monochrome
squatter behind the frothy foam,
birdless, cheerless, monotonous
tenant of the North Sea:
        You own
me, all magic is yours alone,
because no other petty truth
matches the miracle of youth,
grey town!
        Wild geese and misty strand,
for all your marsh-grassy desolation,

sun-deprived vistas, briny smells,
you are my self-defining station
of Calvary, my inspiration,
homeland, memory, elation:
Was I a child anywhere else?

    An elaborate variation on "*Die Stadt*" by Theodor Storm (1817–1888).

AUTUMN DAY

Lord: It is time. The summer was fair.
Rest your shadow on the sundial's face,
Release the autumn breezes in the air.

Order the last grapes to ripen on the vine,
Let them have two more southerly days
As sunlight shimmers, morning frost delays,
And the seed's sweetness yields a weighty wine.

Who is now homeless, will never build a home.
He'll roam in rooms inside a stranger's house.
Wake with a start, write long letters, and browse
In brittle books, then in alleys alone,
Watch the curling leaves whirl without a pause.

A free translation of "*Herbsttag*" by Rainer Maria Rilke (1875–1926).

IBN AMMAR AL-ANDALUSI, 1000 A.D.

The parks, the nights, the naked bodies' blur,
the books, fountains, gold coins in his purse,
the olive trees, mosques, minarets; the myrrh,
the honeyed scent of joy without remorse,
his gem-crusted weapons, his jet-black horse.
In pride he wrote this, because it was clear
within the lustrous balustrades of Seville
all worshipped and quoted him, the Grand Vizier:

"I am Ammar. The fame of my verse flies
over the mountains and the western sea
and from the south a desert wind replies,
only a fool is ignorant of me.
A golden lizard on a golden disc,
if I slither from the lewd lips of a boy
into the eager ear of an odalisque
she leaves her master and becomes my toy.
Nor will this change after my body lies
under an obelisk."

He was cheerful and happier than I,
for when on Spanish domes the arabesque
loosened and fell, he never questioned why,
or why people grew flabby and grotesque,
and did not sense the fabric's fading dye
or in his own tunic the broken thread,
the fountains of the city running dry,
he did not taste the filth inside his bread
or see the boys who knew his poems die
or view the burning library with dread.
Brave and clever, he failed to note the fact

that faith's no help, nor wit, courage, nor dagger,
that no philosophy will resurrect
a culture: collapsing is forever.

A free translation of "*Ibn Ammar Al-Andalusi, 1000 A.D.*"
by George Faludy (1910–2006).

TO A FASCIST DEPUTY

They say you're aging. The sludge in your veins
has put a chokehold on what some call your heart.
One day, friends will wrap your bloated remains
in your country's flag and place them on a cart,
        a velvet-covered caisson, coarse and crass,
behind which a riderless stallion prances,
followed by raised hats and respectful glances
        from the procession behind the horse's ass
in homage to your political stances
your cortège being oblivious to virtue,
decency, taste, and similar nuances.

Fully licensed to wield a dental drill,
had you been merely keen on making shrill
        noises, you had the perfect instrument.
Rather than hone your teeth on politics
you could have stuck to filling cavities
        but didn't, to your nation's frank lament.
Nor were you content to hunt in the decaying
woods, or stick to harmlessly laying,
        as other gentry did, your serving wench.
Now roadside acacias are swaying
in slender-fingered autumn breezes, playing
the harp of Transdanubia from end to end,
        and scatter your memory, like a stench.

The electioneering grin wiped off your face,
made unblinking by stern death, tightly lipped,
        bony fingers clutching your venom's list,

the apt place for you is inside the crypt.
Your hate-filled soul is at home in your corpse
where in dank darkness it greedily craves
  the glory of the sorcerer's apprentice,
till it enters that circle of Inferno
  where spirits of irredentist bent twist,
while winter winds whistle across your grave's
  snow-smudged contours, you miserable dentist.

Faludy's influence permeates *The Jonas Variations*, from which these poems are taken, including the English language poems Jonas wrote in Faludy's manner.

SEA BREEZE

Away from grieving bodies, well-thumbed books,
dour dungeons of disapproving looks,
gardens of jealous gods and jostling vendors,
forbidden fruits and serpents with agendas,
lactating wives, blank pages: Elope
from the relentless cruelty of hope,
growing shadows that end the day,
away! Between the spume and spray
inebriated birds dip and bob freely:
forget French, pick up Swahili.
True, for all their siren calls
sea breezes may play you false.
Ships wreck, isles sink, and sharks devour,
there may be no auspicious hour,
no second place, no honourable mention,
no blue lagoon, swooping birds, no redemption
from playing out existence's grim string —
but listen, listen to the sailors sing.

> A free translation of "*Brise marine*"
> by Stéphane Mallarmé (1842–1898).

REBIRTH

Some feckless, slipshod dilettante
couldn't begin to comprehend
genius, and over-daubed
the masterpiece with heavy hand.

But long years crack the cheap veneer,
the false paint peels, and a splash
of light cleanses the canvas as
blood tints the painted figures' flesh.

So falls our soul's grim grime away
to show in sunset's dying rays
the vital vision of our first,
our formative, our sacred days.

A free translation of "*Возрождение*"
by Alexander Sergeyevich Pushkin (1799–1837).

ACKNOWLEDGEMENTS

The poems in this book came into being over a period of forty-four years, between 1967 and 2011. Some were broadcast or performed at poetry readings, but most had their public debut in print, usually on the pages of literary magazines and scholarly periodicals.

The literary magazines, scholarly periodicals, and anthologies and collections: *Contemporary Literature in Translation*; *Expanding Horizons* (McGraw-Hill); *Kayak*; *Made in Canada* (Oberon Press); *Modern Canadian Verse* (Oxford); *New American and Canadian Poetry* (Beacon Press); *New Wave Canada* (Contact Press); *Notes for a Native Land* (Oberon Press); *PRISM International*; *Quarry*; *Queen's Quarterly*; *Saturday Night*; *Saturday Review*; *The Blasted Pine* (Macmillan); *The Canadian Forum*; *The Malahat Review*; *The New Romans* (Hurtig); *The Penguin Book of Canadian Verse*; *The Tamarack Review*; *Thumbprints* (Peter Martin Associates); and on the CBC radio program, *Anthology*.

Jonas's poetry was published in five volumes: *The Absolute Smile* (1967, House of Anansi Press); *The Happy Hungry Man* (1970, House of Anansi Press); *Cities* (1973, House of Anansi Press); *The East Wind Blows West* (1993, Cacanadadada Press); and *The Jonas Variations: A Literary Seance* (2011, Cormorant Books).

The poems in this book were suggested by Anna Porter, Barbara Amiel and Robyn Sarah from these five volumes. The final selection was made by Marc Côté.

Born in Budapest, George Jonas came to Canada at the age of twenty-one in 1956. Over the next fifty-nine years, he published sixteen books — five of which are poetry — and contributed some 2,500 articles and opinion pieces to newspapers and periodicals in Canada, the US, and the UK. He worked as a radio and television producer for the CBC from 1962 to 1985, married three times, divorced twice, and wrote, produced, and/or directed close to two hundred dramas and docudramas for stage, radio, and television. His awards for writing and producing include an Edgar, two Nellys, a Gabriel, two Geminis, and three National Magazine Awards. He stopped racing motorcycles in his mid-sixties, flying small planes in his seventies, and contributing columns to the *National Post* in his eighties.

Author photograph taken by Angel Guerra